Pearson

Year 3

Grammar and Punctuation

Activity Workbook

Author:
Hannah
Hirst-Dunton

Published by Pearson Education Limited, 80 Strand, London, WC2R 0RL.
www.pearsonschools.co.uk

Text © Pearson Education Limited 2022
Edited by Florence Production Ltd
Designed by Pearson Education Limited 2022
Typeset by Florence Production Ltd
Produced by Florence Production Ltd and Sarah Loader
Original illustrations © Pearson Education Limited 2022
Cover design by Pearson Education Limited 2022

The right of Hannah Hirst-Dunton to be identified as author of this work has been asserted by her in
accordance with the Copyright, Designs and Patents Act 1988.

First published 2022

25 24 23 22
10 9 8 7 6 5 4 3 2 1

British Library Cataloguing in Publication Data
A catalogue record for this book is available from the British Library

ISBN 978 1 292 42499 6

Printed in Slovakia by Neografia

Acknowledgements
Front Cover: Neonic Flower/Shutterstock; Nadya_Art/Shutterstock

The author and publisher would like to thank the following individuals and organisations for permission to
reproduce photographs:

Shutterstock: Olga Utchenko iv, 6, 15, 30, 37, 44, 53, 59, 68; Spreadthesign iv, 6, 15, 30, 37, 44, 53, 59, 68
All other images © Pearson Education Limited

Notes from the publisher
Pearson has robust editorial processes, including answer and fact checks, to ensure the accuracy of the
content in this publication, and every effort is made to ensure this publication is free of errors. We are,
however, only human, and occasionally errors do occur. Pearson is not liable for any misunderstandings that
arise as a result of errors in this publication, but it is our priority to ensure that the content is accurate. If you
spot an error, please do contact us at resourcescorrections@pearson.com so we can make sure it is corrected.

Contents

About this book

This book will help your child to improve their basic literacy skills, fill gaps in learning and increase confidence in a fun and engaging way. It offers a simple, approachable way for you to guide your child through the grammar and punctuation requirements of the National Curriculum.

Your child's mastery of grammar will allow them to express themselves clearly and meet expectations within the whole English curriculum, and beyond!

Grammar and punctuation made clear

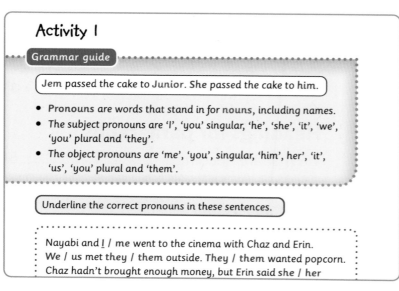

- This activity book is split into bite-sized, manageable topics that are clearly named.
- Each topic is broken down into a number of sessions that develop particular skills and understanding.
- Every session includes grammar or punctuation guides, which give 'at a glance' guidance.

- Then three activities introduce, practise and reinforce the skill focus.
- Completing all three activities in one sitting will help your child get to grips with the concept.
- There are checkpoints for your child to fill in at the end of each topic. This gives you the chance to see where further support is needed.

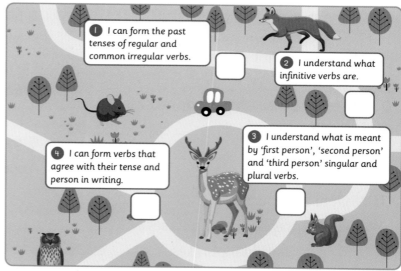

- Short sessions work best. Try setting aside half an hour for your child to explore the three activities.

- Try to complete the topics in the given order, as many of them form key foundations for the ones that follow.

- Your child will ideally work through topics independently, but it's worth being there for when support is needed.

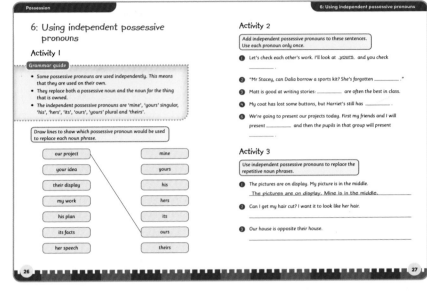

- If your child seems bored or is struggling, suggest they take a break. It might be that they understand the ideas already, or just need time to take something in. They could work on a creative task, such as colouring or following patterns. Try the Pearson Handwriting Activity Workbooks: they contain lots of fun activities, and will also help your child to practise pencil control.

- At the end of a topic, explore the checkpoints with your child and make sure you're happy with what they've understood.

Building from ...

These topics follow on directly from Year 2 to Year 3:

Year 2 topic	Year 3 topic
More determiners	Demonstratives
Expanded noun phrases	Prepositions
Verb forms	Verb forms
Adverbs	Adverbials
Conjunctions and clauses	Conjunctions and clauses
Punctuation	Direct speech Possession

Building towards ...

These topics follow on directly from Year 3 to Year 4:

Year 3 topic	Year 4 topic
Adverbials	Fronted adverbials
Demonstratives	Revising determiners and pronouns
Possession	Understanding 's'
Prepositions	More expanded noun phrases Conjunctions and prepositions for effect
Verb forms	Verb forms for Standard English
Direct speech	Punctuation

Getting started

- Make your child's learning space interesting and fun, in a favourite place to sit or with a favourite toy beside them.
- Encourage your child to step away from any technology or energetic games a little while beforehand, and to take some deep breaths to help them focus.
- Make sure they're sitting comfortably at a table and holding their pencil properly.
- Try to sit with your child to start, even if you're occupied with your own task.

A helping hand

Remind your child to ask for help when they need it. In some topics, you may find they need a little extra guidance. Follow the tips below to support them.

Throughout the topics, children are prompted to consider and say sentences before writing them. Try to take some time to listen to these: an audience could help your child to clarify their ideas.

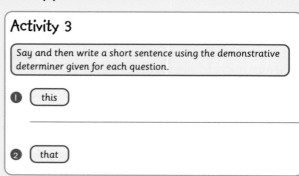

Activity 3

Say and then write a short sentence using the demonstrative determiner given for each question.

❶ (this)

_____

❷ (that)

- Some sentences tell us what someone is saying. This is called <u>speech</u>.
- Speech goes inside speech marks. These are also called inverted commas because they look like upside-down commas.

Underline the speech in these sentences.

❶ Fran says, "<u>It is almost time for lunch.</u>"
❷ Our teacher asked, "Does anyone have the answer?"
❸ Mum shouted, "Come home!"
❹ We called, "Hurry up!"
❺ Enzo said, "It's getting dark already."

Punctuation: What is direct speech? (pages 60–61) and Starting to write speech (pages 62–63)

Speaking to you may also help your child as they learn about direct speech. To firm up understanding, encourage them to say only the speech in the sample sentences.

Demonstratives (pages 7–15) and Possession (pages 16–30)

During these topics, children will draw on the understanding gained in Year 1 **Pronouns** and Year 2 **Determiners**. If possible, you could prompt your child to look back at their earlier work for support.

Grammar guide

Giles shared the cake with Anya. Giles and Anya ate the cake together.
Giles shared the cake with Anya. They ate it together.
This pencil is the pencil I use.   This is the pencil I use.

- Pronouns can stand in for nouns and noun phrases, to avoid repetition.
  - The subject personal pronouns are 'I', 'you' singular, 'she', 'he', 'it', 'we', 'you' plural and 'they'.
  - The object personal pronouns are 'me', 'you' singular, 'her', 'him', 'it', 'us', 'you' plural and 'them'.
- As well as being demonstrative determiners, the words 'this', 'that', 'these' and 'those' can be demonstrative pronouns.

Tricky concepts

Possessive apostrophes

Using possessive apostrophes after 's' trips up even adults! Compare the rules for adding them after singular nouns and plural nouns closely, and ask your child to create their own example phrases.

Adverbials of cause

Some 'cause' adverbials don't give a direct cause but a different kind of reason. For example, 'despite' shows a condition of an event. You could find more examples online to illustrate this.

Prepositions

Prepositions can be part of noun phrases or adverbial phrases. If a phrase that starts with a preposition can be moved around in its sentence, it's likely to be an adverbial phrase.

Technical terms

Even when children know and understand the structures of grammar, terminology can make things seem difficult. Help your child to use the Glossary, which makes the terms clearer.

Progress check

- Once your child has worked on some activities, judge how confident they are with carrying on alone. If they're keen for independence, they're probably on the right track.
- Encourage your child to talk to you about what they are learning. Getting an explanation in their own words will show you how much they've understood.

Extension activities

- While they're looking at their reading materials or unfamiliar texts such as newspapers, challenge your child to spot as many prepositions as they can in one minute. You could repeat this exercise using demonstratives or subordinating conjunctions.
- Some children may spot that some adverbial 'phrases' are actually adverbial clauses. These will be explored in later years, but you could ask your child to note that adverbial clauses always begin with subordinating conjunctions.

Putting grammar and punctuation skills to use

Help your child to understand that their new grammar and punctuation skills are in use everywhere. Encourage them to find examples around them, including in their reading materials.

- Draw your child's attention to topic headings and sub-headings in non-fiction texts. Ask them to explain how these help the reader.
- Point out that play scripts write direct speech in a different way. Challenge your child to rewrite one or two lines using the speech punctuation they have learned.

Adverbials

1: What are adverbials?

Activity 1

Grammar guide

> Jan **quickly kicked** the ball **with all her strength**.
> She was **really proud** when she scored.

- Some adverbials are single words: these are called **adverbs**.
- Others are made up of more than one word: these are called **adverbial phrases**.
- Like an adverb, an adverbial phrase adds information to a **verb** or an **adjective**.

Underline the adverbial phrases.

1. They have a lot of energy <u>in the morning</u>.
2. Frank practises the violin during lunch break.
3. I prepared Gran's surprise party with great excitement.

Activity 2

Grammar guide

- Some adverbials add information about time. They tell us when something happened.
- Some adverbials add information about cause. They tell us why something happened.

Underline the adverbial phrase in each of the following sentences. Write 'time' or 'cause' to show what kind of information it adds.

1. We met each other <u>on Saturday</u>.

2. To stay dry, I use an umbrella.

3. Enzo and Lea spoke <u>every day</u>.

4. The weather at the <u>weekend</u> was awful.

5. I earned a point as a result of my good work.

time ~~saturday~~

cause

time

time

cause

Activity 3

Underline the adverb or adverbial phrase in each of the following sentences.

Write 'adverb' or an 'adverbial phrase' to show what kind of adverbial is in each sentence.

Then circle the verb or adjective it describes.

1. Mathias (looked) up <u>with a frown</u>.

_____

2. We cycled to school in quite a rush.

_____

3. The sky was bright pink at sunset.

_____

4. The shop was surprisingly busy.

_____

2: Adding adverbials

Activity 1

> **Grammar guide**
>
> - An adverbial can add information to an adjective or a verb.
> - An adverbial can be a single word (an adverb) or a longer phrase (an adverbial phrase).

1 Add one of these adverbial phrases to each sentence.

for his birthday	every day
to cheer him up	last week

a I visited him.

I visited him _to cheer him up_

_____

b Dean's grandpa gave him a present.

_____

_____

2 Look again at the four adverbial phrases above. Write down the two that are adverbials of cause.

_____

_____

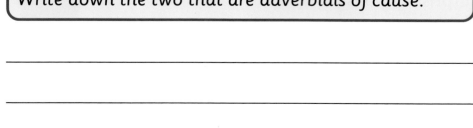

Activity 2

Change each sentence to include an adverbial of your choice. Use at least one adverbial of cause and at least one adverbial of time.

1 She realised that she wasn't nervous.

_____

_____

2 Jordan wasn't at school.

_____

_____

3 Zoey sat down and began to eat.

_____

_____

Activity 3

1 Write a sentence about sport that includes an adverb.

_____

_____

2 Write a sentence about reading that includes an adverbial phrase.

_____

_____

What do I Know?

1 I know what an adverbial phrase is.

2 I know the difference between adverbial phrases of time and adverbial phrases of cause.

3 I can choose an adverbial phrase and add it to a sentence.

4 I can write a sentence that includes an adverbial.

6

1: What are demonstrative determiners?

Activity 1

Grammar guide

> I'd like **some breakfast**. Please pass **a piece of toast** and **the jam**.
> I don't want **any cereal** but I'd like **one of the muffins**.

- **Determiners**, including articles, begin both simple and expanded <u>noun phrases</u>.
- They give basic information about the noun. This could be about the number of things and whether something is one of many ('indefinite') or a particular thing ('definite').
- The words 'a', 'an' and 'some' are **indefinite articles. Other determiners can also be indefinite.**
- The word 'the' is the **definite** article. **Other determiners can also be definite.**

Tick the sentences that include definite determiners.

- We are close to the station now. ✓
- Some children grow vegetables themselves. ☐
- Any teacher can review your work. ☐
- All of the boxes were used. ☐
- I cycle but the other pupils walk. ☐

Activity 2

I found **these** books in **this** box, and you found **those** books in **that** box.

Demonstrative determiners point out (demonstrate) particular things.
- The words 'this' and 'that' point out things that are singular.
- The words 'these' and 'those' point out things that are plural.
- The words 'this' and 'these' point out things that are nearby.
- The words 'that' and 'those' point out things that are further away.

Underline the demonstrative determiners. Tick two boxes to show the kind of thing that each of them points out.

1 <u>These</u> donations will pay for new books. ☐ singular ☑ near ☑ plural ☐ far

2 Those teams will meet in the final. ☐ singular ☐ near ☐ plural ☐ far

3 We were saving that chocolate! ☐ singular ☐ near ☐ plural ☐ far

4 This pen is leaking everywhere. ☐ singular ☐ near ☐ plural ☐ far

Activity 3

Underline all the demonstrative determiners.

The articles in <u>this</u> week's school newspaper show the wonderful things pupils have been doing. These children grew vegetables in the school garden. That potato they're holding is huge! Some other children set up a writing group. I wonder if they'll write about those giant potatoes!

2: Using demonstrative determiners

Activity 1

Grammar guide

Demonstrative determiners point out (demonstrate) particular things.

- The words 'this' and 'that' point out things that are singular.
- The words 'these' and 'those' point out things that are plural.
- The words 'this' and 'these' point out things that are nearby.
- The words 'that' and 'those' point out things that are further away.

Look at this sentence.

The farmer crossed the field to look at the sheep.

1. Add a demonstrative determiner that would point out one sheep, nearby.

   The farmer crossed the field to look at __this__ sheep.

2. Add a demonstrative determiner that would point out one sheep, far away.

   The farmer crossed the field to look at _____ sheep.

3. Add a demonstrative determiner that would point out several sheep, nearby.

   The farmer crossed the field to look at _____ sheep.

4. Add a demonstrative determiner that would point out several sheep, far away.

   The farmer crossed the field to look at _____ sheep.

Activity 2

Add the correct demonstrative determiner to each sentence.

1 _These_ heavy bags are straining my arms!

2 Horace is the boy over there, in _____ armchair.

3 I'm sharing out _____ soup between the four of us.

4 Could you pass me _____ plant pots, please?

Activity 3

Say and then write a short sentence using the demonstrative determiner given for each question.

1 this

_____

2 that

_____

3 these

_____

4 those

_____

3: What are demonstrative pronouns?

Activity 1

Grammar guide

> Giles shared the cake with Anya. **Giles and Anya** ate **the cake** together.
> Giles shared the cake with Anya. **They** ate **it** together.
> **This** pencil is the pencil I use.   **This** is the pencil I use.

- **Pronouns** can stand in for **nouns** and **noun phrases**, to avoid repetition.
  - The subject personal pronouns are 'I', 'you' singular, 'she', 'he', 'it', 'we', 'you' plural and 'they'.
  - The object personal pronouns are 'me', 'you' singular, 'her', 'him', 'it', 'us', 'you' plural and 'them'.
- As well as being **demonstrative determiners**, the words 'this', 'that', 'these' and 'those' can be **demonstrative pronouns**.
  - 'This' and 'that' point out things that are singular.
  - 'These' and 'those' point out things that are plural.
  - 'This' and 'these' point out things that are nearby.
  - 'That' and 'those' point out things that are further away.

> Underline the pronouns and the nouns they replace.
> The nouns may be part of noun phrases that are replaced.

1. The <u>paintings</u> here are beautiful. All of <u>these</u> deserve awards.
2. Jared saw a film and he enjoyed it.
3. This is the best book that I've read in a while.
4. Misaki and Miu wanted to play so Karen passed the ball to them.
5. I thought that was an exciting end to the story.
6. There were sweets hidden in the cupboard, but Geni hadn't found those.

Activity 2

Rewrite each sentence. Replace the demonstrative pronoun with the correct noun phrase.

1 That was a good idea.

That idea was a good idea.

2 Most jumpers are too short for me, but this fits okay.

3 Fran made many of the models, but Jake made those.

4 These are the biscuits we made in class today.

Activity 3

Grammar guide

I took **two** sweets. There were plenty of sweets so I took **two**.

Other words used as **determiners** can be **pronouns**, too.

Underline the pronouns and the nouns or noun phrases they replace.

1 The stew looked tasty so Cary had some.

2 Isaac had finished his tasks but Theo hadn't done any.

3 There's soup or pasta for lunch, and neither contains meat.

4: Using demonstrative pronouns

Activity 1

- The demonstratives 'this', 'that', 'these' and 'those' can be determiners or pronouns.
- They can give basic information about whether something is singular or plural and nearby or far away.

Complete each sentence with the best demonstrative pronoun.

1 There's a really strange beetle over here.

Come here and look at __this_____!

2 I need to find something soft.

Can you see anything like _____?

3 Do you have all the coloured pens?

You'll need _____ for the next lesson.

4 I've selected three drawings.

Can you see what's special about _____?

Activity 2

Rewrite the following sentences. Use demonstrative pronouns instead of repeating the noun phrases.

1 If I carry these dishes, can you carry those dishes?

If I carry these dishes, can you carry those?

2 I know you wanted Aimee's book, but read this book instead.

3 Everyone needs a paint brush. Can you hand out these paint brushes?

4 John had a great idea – I wish I had thought of the great idea.

Activity 3

Complete each sentence with an appropriate pronoun from the words below.

most	none	plenty	much	one	some

1 You have loads of sandwiches – can I have _____?

2 Some pupils voted for Nick, but _____ voted for Rani.

3 Paula has lots of homework but her sister doesn't have _____.

What do I know?

1. I can identify the four demonstrative determiners.

2. I know that a demonstrative determiner shows whether something is singular or plural and near or far.

4. I understand that 'this', 'that', 'these' and 'those' can be pronouns as well as determiners.

3. I can use demonstrative determiners to show whether something is singular or plural and near or far.

5. I understand how demonstrative pronouns can be used.

6. I can use demonstrative pronouns to show whether something is singular or plural and near or far.

1: Exploring more possessive nouns

Activity 1

Punctuation guide

> The **car owned by Jules** was the **winner of the race**.
> **Jules's car** was the **race's winner**.

- Possession means that **something belongs to someone or something else**. It could be **owned by them** or **related to them in a different way**.
- A singular possessive noun is made up of the noun plus **apostrophe and 's'**.
- If a singular noun ends in 's', add an **apostrophe and then another 's'**.

Change each phrase to use a possessive noun.

1 the kitten owned by Marc   _Marc's kitten_

2 the clothes worn by my brother   _____

3 the highest peak of the mountain   _____

Activity 2

Punctuation guide

> The clothes for **girls** cost less than the clothes for **women**.
> The **girls'** clothes cost less than the **women's** clothes.

- A **plural noun that ends in 's'** takes an **apostrophe** but no extra 's' when it is possessive.
- A **plural noun that does not end in 's'** takes an **apostrophe and 's'** when it is possessive.

1 For each sentence, write down the two owners and the two things belonging to them.

a The children's laughter caught their parents' attention.

Owners: _____children_____ _____

Things belonging to them: __laughter_____ _____

b The jugglers' balls landed at the men's feet.

Owners: _____ _____

Things belonging to them: _____ _____

2 Change each of the underlined phrases to include a possessive noun.

a The skill of the doctors saved the lives of those men.

____The doctors' skill saved those men's lives.____

b The workbooks of the children were in the cupboards of the teachers.

_____

Activity 3

Change the sentence to use two possessive nouns.

The ability of grass to get nutrients is improved by tunnels made by earthworms.

_____

_____

_____

2: Spotting possessive pronouns

Activity 1

Grammar guide

Jem passed the cake to **Junior**. **She** passed the cake to **him**.

- **Pronouns** are words that stand in for **nouns**, including names.
- The subject pronouns are 'I', 'you' singular, 'he', 'she', 'it', 'we', 'you' plural and 'they'.
- The object pronouns are 'me', 'you', singular, 'him', her', 'it', 'us', 'you' plural and 'them'.

Underline the correct pronouns in these sentences.

Nayabi and **I** / **me** went to the cinema with Chaz and Erin. **We** / **us** met **they** / **them** outside. **They** / **them** wanted popcorn. Chaz hadn't brought enough money, but Erin said **she** / **her** would get some and share it with **he** / **him**.

Activity 2

Grammar guide

- Possessive pronouns stand in for possessive nouns.
- There are two types of possessive pronouns to learn.
- The words 'my', 'your', 'his', 'her', 'its', 'our' and 'their' are possessive pronouns that are used as determiners.
- The words 'mine', 'yours', 'his', 'hers', 'its', 'ours' and 'theirs' are possessive pronouns used independently. This means that they are used on their own.

Use the information in the grammar guides to fill in this table with the object pronouns and possessive pronouns. You can refer to it later.

	Subject pronouns	Object pronouns	Possessive pronouns	
			Determiners	Independent pronouns
Singular	I	me	my	mine
	you			
	he			
	she			
	it			
Plural	we			
	you			
	they			

Activity 3

Underline all the possessive pronouns, including the possessive determiners.

Sadie was judging our cakes, because it was her idea to hold the contest. Ours both looked tasty: I could see my cake was smaller than yours, but your cake had less icing than mine. Max thought his was best. Mae and Mo baked their entry together, though, and theirs won. It looked delicious!

3: What are possessive determiners?

Activity 1

Grammar guide

> There are <u>three</u> <u>different fruits</u> in <u>the bowl</u>. You can have <u>any fruit</u>.

- **Determiners** begin <u>noun phrases</u>.
- They can give basic information about the noun. This could be about **number** and about whether something is **definite** (particular) or **indefinite** (general).

> Underline all the determiners.

I am not sure what to do with <u>all of the</u> old toys. I think I should give some games to charity. There are two dolls and a teddy my sister might like. Maybe I'll keep a few things, too.

Activity 2

Grammar guide

> **Our** coats are lots of different colours. This is **my** yellow coat, and that's **your** black coat. **Her** coat is green. **His** coat is red, with white on **its** hood. **Their** coats are blue.

- **Possessive pronouns** show that something belongs to someone or something else. This could mean that it is owned by them or is related to them in a different way.
- Some possessive pronouns are used as determiners. This means they are used before nouns.
- The words 'my', 'your' singular, 'his', 'her', 'its', 'our', 'your' plural and 'their' are **possessive determiners**.

1 Underline the possessive pronouns that are determiners.

"<u>Our</u> bus will be waiting!" Nadia shouted to Pietr. "Have you seen my bag?"

"I saw it in your bedroom," he called. His voice sounded annoyed.

Tammie and Jack were waiting on the bus for their friends. The driver of the bus opened its doors. Ignoring her frown, Nadia and Pietr got on.

2 Draw lines to show what each possessive determiner in the story means.

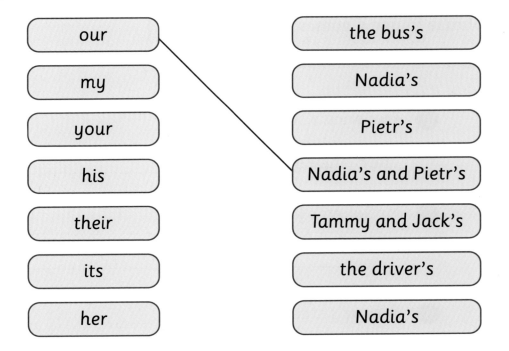

our	the bus's
my	Nadia's
your	Pietr's
his	Nadia's and Pietr's
their	Tammy and Jack's
its	the driver's
her	Nadia's

Activity 3

Look again at the story in Activity 2.

1 If the possessive pronouns are standing in for singular possessive nouns, underline them again.

2 If they are standing in for plural possessive nouns, circle them.

4: Using possessive determiners

Activity 1

Grammar guide

- Possessive pronouns show that something belongs to someone or something else. This could mean it is owned by them or is related to them in a different way.
- Some possessive pronouns are used as determiners.
- The words 'my', 'your' singular, 'his', 'its, 'our', 'your' plural and 'their' are possessive determiners.

Change each phrase to use a possessive pronoun as a determiner.

1 Frederica's shoes

her shoes

2 Mr Salieri's lesson plan

3 the car's steering wheel

Activity 2

> Add possessive pronouns as determiners in these sentences.
> Use each pronoun only once.

① Doc put on ___his___ scarf and handed Wendy _____ hat.

② The birds cheerfully sang _____ songs.

③ The spider spun _____ web.

④ Derick and I really enjoyed _____ day together.

⑤ Thank you so much for _____ kind wishes on _____ birthday.

Activity 3

> Change the underlined words to noun phrases that include a possessive determiner.

① Get out <u>the crayons belonging to you and the other children</u>.

  Get out your crayons.

② The judges announced <u>the decision that they had made</u>.

_____

③ This is <u>the house where my family and I live</u>.

_____

5: What are independent possessive pronouns?

Activity 1

What was **that** noise? Did you hear **that**?
I've had **one** cookie. Would you like **one**?

Some words can be used as both **determiners** and **pronouns**.

Underline the pronouns.

Carl and Carrie had baked some biscuits. There were <u>loads</u>, but the children had none to spare. The biscuits were for a charity bake sale at school.
"Please help me carry these!" Carl called. "Don't eat any, though!"

Activity 2

This painting is **mine**. That one is **yours**. I think my favourite is **his**, but **hers** is also good. **Its** colours are nice and bright. Miss Terence says **ours** are all great. Next she will visit Class 2 and judge **theirs**.

- Some **possessive pronouns** are used independently. This means that they are used on their own.
- They replace both a possessive noun and the noun for the thing that is owned.
- The independent possessive pronouns are 'mine', 'yours' singular, 'his', 'hers, 'ours', 'yours' plural and 'theirs'.

❶ Underline the independent possessive pronouns. Do not underline any possessive determiners.

"Could we borrow your book?" Sheila and Dom asked. "Ours are at home."

"Why mine?" Ginny replied. "Could you ask Tim and Sun-Yin for theirs?"

"Their books are both old," Sheila frowned. "His is torn and hers has pages missing. Yours is new."

❷ Look again at the story above. Draw lines to show what each possessive determiner in the story means.

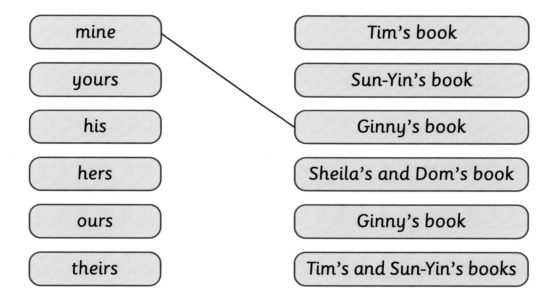

mine	Tim's book
yours	Sun-Yin's book
his	Ginny's book
hers	Sheila's and Dom's book
ours	Ginny's book
theirs	Tim's and Sun-Yin's books

Activity 3

Look again at the story in Activity 2.

❶ If the possessive pronouns are standing in for singular possessive nouns, underline them again.

❷ If the possessive pronouns are standing in for plural possessive nouns, circle them.

6: Using independent possessive pronouns

Activity 1

Grammar guide

- Some possessive pronouns are used independently. This means that they are used on their own.
- They replace both a possessive noun and the noun for the thing that is owned.
- The independent possessive pronouns are 'mine', 'yours' singular, 'his', 'hers', 'its', 'ours', 'yours' plural and 'theirs'.

Draw lines to show which possessive pronoun would be used to replace each noun phrase.

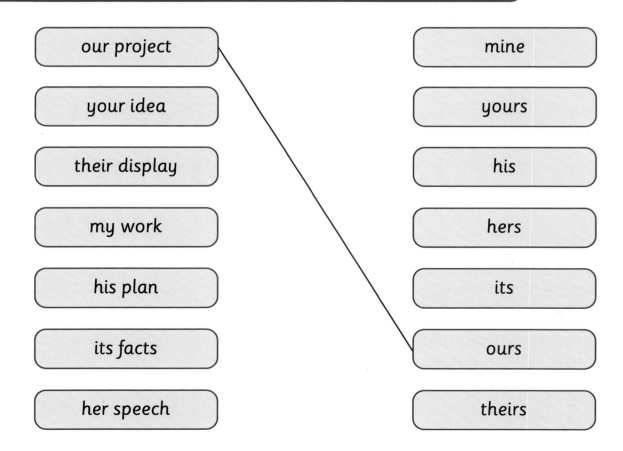

our project	mine
your idea	yours
their display	his
my work	hers
his plan	its
its facts	ours
her speech	theirs

Activity 2

Add independent possessive pronouns to these sentences.
Use each pronoun only once.

1 Let's check each other's work. I'll look at __yours__ and you check

_____ .

2 "Mr Stacey, can Dalia borrow a sports kit? She's forgotten _____ ."

3 Matt is good at writing stories: _____ are often the best in class.

4 My coat has lost some buttons, but Harriet's still has _____ .

5 We're going to present our projects today. First my friends and I will

present _____ and then the pupils in that group will present

_____ .

Activity 3

Use independent possessive pronouns to replace the
repetitive noun phrases.

1 The pictures are on display. My picture is in the middle.

   __The pictures are on display. Mine is in the middle.__

2 Can I get my hair cut? I want it to look like her hair.

_____

3 Our house is opposite their house.

_____

7: Choosing possessive pronouns

Activity 1

Grammar guide

- Possessive pronouns stand in for possessive nouns.
- Some possessive pronouns can be used as determiners, at the beginning of a noun phrase.
- Some possessive pronouns can be used independently, to represent a whole noun phrase.

Complete this table from memory.

	Subject pronouns	Object pronouns	Possessive pronouns	
			Determiners	Independent pronouns
Singular	I	me	my	mine
	you			
	he			
	she			
	it			
Plural	we			
	you			
	they			

Activity 2

Underline the **correct** possessive pronouns in the sentences.

1. Abena can't find <u>her</u> / hers hat. Are you sure that one is your / yours?

2. Mine / My sunflower grew taller than their / theirs bean plant.

3. We couldn't decide whose house to go to: my / mine or her / hers.

4. Jina has always been your / yours friend – and now she's our / ours, too.

5. In drama, I think our / ours script is much funnier than their / theirs.

Activity 3

1. Write one sentence that uses 'its' as a possessive determiner.

_____

_____

_____

2. Write one sentence that uses 'his' as an independent possessive pronoun.

_____

_____

_____

What do I Know?

1 I understand how to punctuate singular and plural possessive nouns that end in different ways.

2 I can identify the possessive pronouns that are used as determiners and that are used independently.

4 I can use possessive determiners to show belonging.

3 I can identify what possessive determiners mean.

5 I can identify what independent possessive pronouns mean.

6 I can use independent possessive pronouns to stand in for noun phrases and avoid repeating words.

7 I can identify all possessive pronouns and use them in sentences.

1: What are prepositions?

Activity 1

The tree is tall. The <u>green</u> leaves grow.

- A noun phrase is a noun and the other words that add information to it, which together act as a noun in a sentence.
- A **simple noun phrase** is just a determiner and a noun.
- Adding an <u>adjective</u> to a simple noun phrase makes it longer and more detailed. The phrase becomes an **expanded noun phrase**.

Underline all of the noun phrases.
Circle the simple noun phrases.

When I was <u>a very young child</u>, (my grandfather) kept an enormous sweet jar in his kitchen. There were some toffees, chewy mints and bright red lollipops.

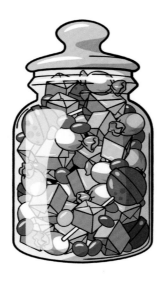

Activity 2

Grammar guide

the **book with** <u>the blue cover</u>
the marathon **in aid of** <u>charity</u>

- In a noun phrase, **prepositions** can link a **noun** or pronoun to other <u>information that describes it</u>.
- Prepositions can be single words or short phrases.

Circle the preposition in each sentence. Underline the whole of the noun phrase it expands.

1 I was late for <u>the lesson</u> (at) 9 o'clock.

2 The man with the long white beard is Mae's uncle.

3 Gloria enjoyed the food at her local restaurant.

4 We all enjoyed our day off due to snow.

5 Her time up to noon was spent gardening.

Activity 3

Tick the sentence in each pair that uses the correct preposition.

1 The film about sea monsters was my favourite. ◯
   The film in sea monsters was my favourite. ◯

2 The fish on the tank swam up to the surface. ◯
   The fish in the tank swam up to the surface. ◯

3 Mr Jones was accepting donations under the school trip. ◯
   Mr Jones was accepting donations for the school trip. ◯

2: What are prepositional phrases?

Activity 1

Grammar guide

Please use **the chair <u>in the corner</u>**.

- **Noun phrases** can be expanded using <u>prepositional phrases</u>.
- These are linked to the noun using a **preposition**.

Underline the prepositional phrase in each sentence.

1. I read the new book <u>by my favourite author</u>.
2. Kate didn't share Leah's interest in tennis.
3. The buses on Sundays always ran late.
4. The chattering noise of the audience ended suddenly.

Activity 2

Underline each expanded noun phrase that includes a prepositional phrase. There is one in each sentence.

1. Sun had a letter from his cousin <u>the day before yesterday</u>.
2. Digby froze when he saw the bared teeth of the snarling tiger.
3. I was blinded for a moment by the bright, flashing reflection in the window of the house.
4. After the move, Bibi had to go to a new school far from her friends.
5. Your whispers during the film were annoying.

Activity 3

Look again at the expanded noun phrases you underlined in Activity 2.

Write them as simple noun phrases of just two words.

Think about how much detail has been lost.

① <u>the day</u>

② _____

③ _____

④ _____

⑤ _____

3: Using prepositional phrases

Activity 1

Shall we sit on **the wooden bench facing the sun?**
Shall we sit on the **wooden bench** <u>facing the sun</u>?

- **Noun phrases** can be expanded by **adjectives** before the **nouns** and <u>prepositional phrases</u> after the **nouns**.
- **Prepositions** begin prepositional phrases.

Complete the paragraph using the following prepositions.
Use each preposition only once.

of	for	through	in	on	at

Tim found his way ___through___ the corridor and entered

the door _____ the sitting room. The fire

_____ the grate was crackling and the clock

_____ the mantelpiece chimed. This was the last

room Tim could explore in his hunt _____ the

legendary treasure. He had to succeed before his departure

_____ dawn.

Activity 2

Rewrite the paragraph, using adjectives and prepositional phrases to expand the underlined noun phrases.

A man appeared suddenly in the doorway. He carried a satchel, and a parrot was perched on his shoulder. When he spoke, we heard a croaky voice. He asked for our help.

An old man with a long beard

_____

_____

_____

_____

_____

_____

Activity 3

Read the paragraph you wrote in Activity 2. Are any of the extra details confusing? Could you add any more descriptive information? Write any changes you want to make.

_____

_____

_____

_____

What do I Know?

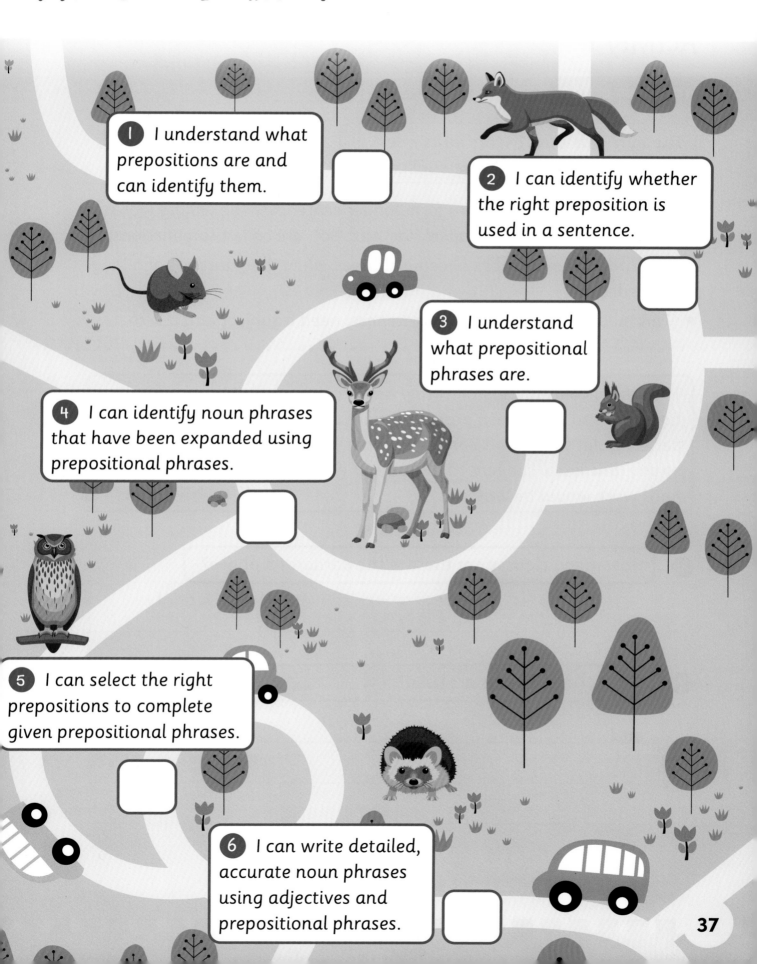

1 I understand what prepositions are and can identify them.

2 I can identify whether the right preposition is used in a sentence.

3 I understand what prepositional phrases are.

4 I can identify noun phrases that have been expanded using prepositional phrases.

5 I can select the right prepositions to complete given prepositional phrases.

6 I can write detailed, accurate noun phrases using adjectives and prepositional phrases.

37

1: Revising clauses and conjunctions

Activity 1

> The <u>sun</u> *was* out. <u>I</u> *wore* sunscreen.
> The <u>sun</u> *was* out so <u>I</u> *wore* sunscreen.

- **Sentences** can be linked to form longer sentences. The linking words, such as 'and', 'but', 'because', 'or' and 'so', are called conjunctions.
- The **original sentences** become **clauses** when they are part of a longer sentence.
- This means that clauses, like sentences, need a <u>subject</u> and a *verb*.

> The school concert was tomorrow and Edi was really nervous. She had a solo so she'd been practising hard for weeks. She could play it perfectly but she wasn't confident about performing because she was so shy. She knew she had to overcome her fears, though, or all of her hard work would be wasted.

1 How many clauses are there in the paragraph above?

_____

2 Which conjunctions are used?

and, _____

_____

_____

Activity 2

> I opened the curtains **and** I looked out of the window.
> I tried to open the window **but** I couldn't **because** it was stuck.
> I wanted to fix it **so** I needed to fetch the tools or to use some oil.

Different conjunctions create different kinds of connections:

- 'And' connects similar ideas.
- 'But' connects contrasting ideas.
- 'Because' introduces a reason.
- 'So' introduces an effect.
- 'Or' links two possibilities. Only one of them can happen or be true.

> Write five short sentences, using one of these conjunctions to link your ideas in each sentence. Use each conjunction only once.

| and | but | because | so | or |

1. I wanted to stay up but I'm too tired.
2. _____
3. _____
4. _____
5. _____

Activity 3

> Look again at the sentences you wrote for Activity 2. Underline each clause.

2: More subordinating conjunctions

Activity 1

Grammar guide

> It was bright but it was cold. The snow fell so I made a snowman.
> It was cold but it was bright. I made a snowman so the snow fell.

- A **main clause** gives the main point in a sentence.
- A **subordinate clause** gives extra information that is not the key point.
- There can be more than one **main clause** if they are equally important.
- Swapping the order of **main clauses** does not affect meaning.
- Swapping a **main clause** and a **subordinate clause** does affect it.

Tick the sentences that include subordinate clauses.

- I'd left my bag at home so I had to return for it. ✓
- The desert's sun is blazing hot but it is cold at night. ☐
- Would you like to eat out or would you prefer to cook? ☐
- Dina was keen to finish the game because she'd almost won. ☐
- Grandma went to get groceries and Jamal tidied the house. ☐

Activity 2

Grammar guide

> We were tired **and** we were hungry.
> We were hungry <u>**so**</u> we had lunch. We had lunch <u>**because**</u> we were hungry.
> We had a picnic <u>**where**</u> we found benches. We have been here <u>**since**</u> we ate.

- Main clauses are linked by **coordinating conjunctions** such as 'and'.
- Main and subordinate clauses are linked by <u>subordinating conjunctions</u>.
- The conjunctions '**so**' and '**because**' are subordinating conjunctions.
- Other subordinating conjunctions include the words '**where**' and '**when**'.
- Some words that are **prepositions** can also be subordinating conjunctions.

Use these subordinating conjunctions to complete the sentences. Use each of them only once.

1. I'm not going to be here for the party <u>although</u> I'd love to go.
2. You can borrow Kwame's laptop _____ you're careful with it.
3. Zane had broken his promise _____ Kara no longer trusted him.
4. I'll return the library book _____ I find it.
5. Abi and Ada became friends _____ they met at the drama group.

Activity 3

Each of these sentences contains a word that is a preposition. In each example, underline the sentence in which it is used as a conjunction.

1. There was a school quiz the day before yesterday. I had studied before I took part.
2. My final class today is the lesson after this. I have work to do after I get home, though.

3: Writing subordinate clauses

Activity 1

> I've liked Joshua since we first met.
> We first met since I've liked Joshua.

- A **subordinate clause** contains information that relies on a **main clause** for meaning.
- Swapping a **main clause** and a **subordinate clause** around a **conjunction** changes the meaning of the sentence or makes no sense.

Add a subordinate clause to complete each sentence.

1 Joni was nervous because <u>she had to give a speech.</u>

2 I'll meet you when _____

3 We waited until _____

Activity 2

Write three sentences of your own, using three different subordinating conjunctions to link your ideas. You can use some of the conjunctions below, or others.

where	because	unless	before	as	though

1 _____

_____

2 _____

_____

3 _____

_____

Activity 3

Choose one of the sentences you wrote in Activity 2. Write the main clause again, but add a different subordinating conjunction and a different subordinate clause.

_____

_____

_____

What do I Know?

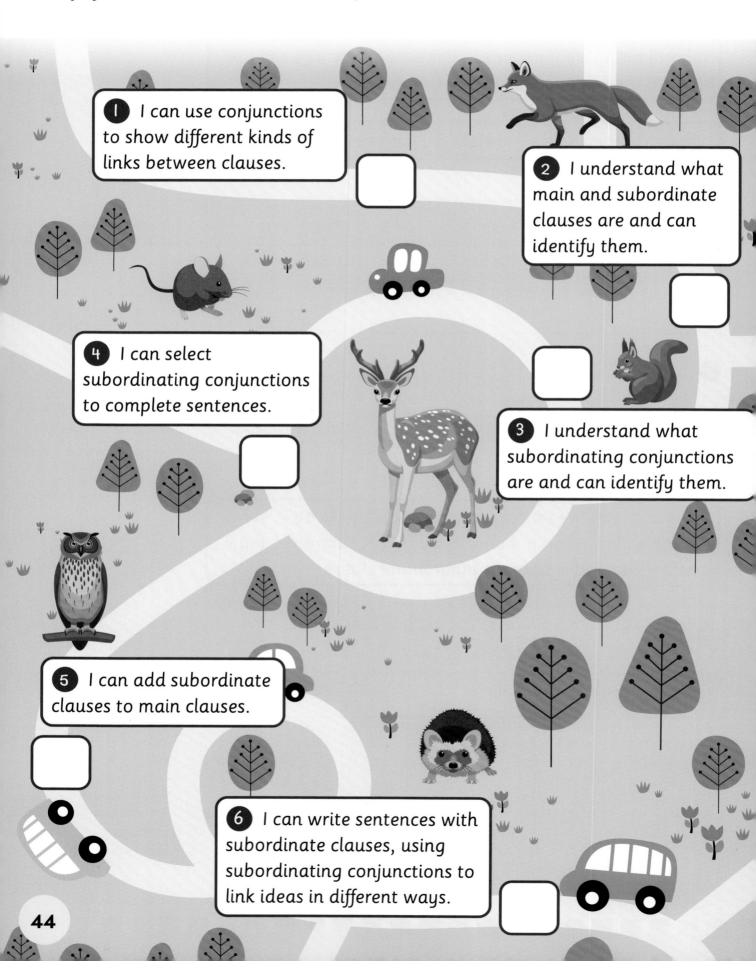

1 I can use conjunctions to show different kinds of links between clauses.

2 I understand what main and subordinate clauses are and can identify them.

4 I can select subordinating conjunctions to complete sentences.

3 I understand what subordinating conjunctions are and can identify them.

5 I can add subordinate clauses to main clauses.

6 I can write sentences with subordinate clauses, using subordinating conjunctions to link ideas in different ways.

1: Exploring simple tenses

Activity 1

Grammar guide

> I **look** at a picture. You **copy** it. You **match** them up.
> We **enjoy** both but **prefer** yours.
> Kayla **looks** at a picture. Ben **copies** it. He **matches** them up.
> She **enjoys** both but **prefers** Ben's.
> We **looked** at a picture. We **copied** it. We **matched** them up.
> We **enjoyed** both but **preferred** yours.

- Verbs change depending on their subject and tense.
- The spellings of **regular verbs** change according to their endings.

> Ben **won** the contest. I **was** happy that he **had** the prize.
> Ben **wins** the contest. I **am** happy that he **has** the prize.

- However, some verbs are irregular. Many have **irregular past tenses**.
- The verbs 'be' and 'have' also have **irregular present tenses**.

Write the past-tense form of each present-tense verb.

1 I <u>make</u> tea.   made _____

2 He <u>cooks</u> dinner for his family.   _____

3 You <u>hurry</u>.   _____

4 They <u>trace</u> the outlines carefully.   _____

5 She <u>travels</u>.   _____

6 We <u>are</u> here.   _____

Activity 2

to walk

- An **infinitive verb** is the root verb: the word 'to' followed by the verb's basic form.
- The infinitive form expresses no tense and no person.

Write the infinitive form of each irregular past-tense verb.

1 He <u>was</u> here.   <u>to be</u>   **2** They <u>had</u> it.   _____

3 It <u>went</u> away.   _____   **4** You all <u>came</u>.   _____

5 I <u>found</u> it.   _____   **6** You <u>flew</u> alone.   _____

7 We <u>slept</u> heavily.   _____   **8** She <u>spoke</u> up.   _____

Activity 3

I walk. You walk. She walks. He walks. It walks.
We walk. You walk. They walk.
I walk. You walk. She walks. He walks. It walks.
We walk. You walk. They walk.

- Verbs and their subjects can be described as **singular** or **plural**.
- They can also be described as **first person**, **second person** or **third person**.

Look back at Activity 2. Work out which 'person' each sentence uses. Add labels to the sentences.

2: Practising verb agreement

Activity 1

Grammar guide

Verbs must always agree with their person and with the tense of the sentence.

Underline all the verbs that are not in the correct person or tense.

The mystery <u>begin</u> weeks ago, when Hayak returned from school to saw strangers in his kitchen. They talks to his mother for hours, and then leave the house silently. Now, things seem strange: teachers was kinder, and his friends did not know what to say.

Activity 2

1 Rewrite the paragraph using the past tense.

I know it is your birthday, so I plan ahead and go to your party. You have such a surprise, which makes me smile.

I knew _____

_____

_____

2 Rewrite the paragraph using the present tense and the third person singular: 'she'.

My dream was this: I met my grandfather, and he said he had an adventure ahead of him. Then he rose into the air and flew.

Her dream is _____

_____

_____

Activity 3

Change each underlined infinitive verb to its correct tense and person.

Last week, I <u>to forget</u> my gym kit and <u>to skip</u> playing basketball. There <u>to be</u> a game today, and I <u>to be</u> nervous because I <u>to make</u> the mistake of missing practice. Despite this, our coach <u>to say</u> my mistake <u>to do</u> not need to worry me.

Last week, I _____ my gym kit and _____ playing

basketball. There _____ a game today, and I _____

nervous because I _____ the mistake of missing practice.

Despite this, our coach _____ my mistake _____ not

need to worry me.

3: What are perfect tenses?

Activity 1

Grammar guide

> We looked. I **have looked**. She **has looked**.
> We **had looked**.

- Perfect verb forms are used to describe perfectly complete actions.
- They are created using two verbs.
- A helper verb comes first. This is called an **auxiliary verb**. Perfect tenses use the **auxiliary verb** 'to **have**'.
- The second verb names the action. In perfect tenses, this verb form is called a **past participle**.
- Many **past participles** are the same as the verb's past tense.

> Circle the auxiliary verbs. Underline the past participles.

1. We (have) <u>talked</u>.

2. You had recovered.

3. He has been happy.

4. We began the party once Ruhi had arrived.

5. Mum was here, but now she has left.

Activity 2

Grammar guide

We looked. I **have** looked. She **has** looked. We **had** looked.

- Present-perfect verbs use the **present form of the auxiliary verb**: 'have' or 'has'.
- Past-perfect verbs use the **past form of the auxiliary verb**: 'had'.

Underline the perfect verbs. Note whether each is present perfect or past perfect.

1 Juno <u>has caught</u> the ball and is about to throw it. <u>present perfect</u>

2 When she had finished work, Talia drove home. _____

3 I went to collect water but the well had frozen. _____

4 Idris has known Ken since Ken was a baby. _____

5 Kamal has worn the same glasses for years. _____

Activity 3

Tick the sentences that use perfect verbs correctly. Underline the mistakes in the other sentences.

- I have heard his new song. ⬜
- They are come to watch the movie. ⬜
- I had forgotten about the test. ⬜
- We have run all the way here. ⬜
- We had a cat when I was younger. ⬜
- Lida had hoped for a new bike. ⬜

4: Forming perfect verbs

Activity 1

Fill the gap in each sentence with a suitable present participle.

1 I have <u>finished</u> my work now.

2 I had _____ earlier than everyone else.

3 I have _____ to school today.

4 I had _____ to tidy my room but I forgot.

Activity 2

Rewrite the following sentences.

a Basia arrives. She waves to us.

b I was waiting for a train. It rained all night.

1 Use the present-perfect tense.

a <u>Basia has arrived.</u>

b _____

_____

2 Use the past-perfect tense.

a _____

b _____

_____

Activity 3

1 Write a short sentence in the past-perfect tense using the past participle of 'to be'.

_____

_____

2 Write a short sentence in the present-perfect tense using the past participle of 'to say'.

_____

_____

What do I know?

1. I can form the past tenses of regular and common irregular verbs.

2. I understand what infinitive verbs are.

3. I understand what is meant by 'first person', 'second person' and 'third person' singular and plural verbs.

4. I can form verbs that agree with their tense and person in writing.

5. I understand what past perfect and present perfect verb forms are, and how they are formed.

6. I can form present-perfect and past-perfect verbs, and use them in writing.

1: What are headings?

Activity 1

Grammar guide

- Headings are words that appear as titles above pieces of writing.
- A heading tells the reader straight away what a piece of writing will be about.
- Some pieces of writing also have sub-headings. These are smaller titles that appear before paragraphs.
- A paragraph is a group of sentences about similar things.
- Sub-headings can help guide a reader through a piece of writing.

Preparing to Perform on Stage

Before the big day
Make sure you know what you're doing! Being prepared will make you more confident. The key is to practise, whether you're learning your lines for a play, rehearsing your dance moves or learning about a class project.

The day itself!
Try to make sure you've had a good night's sleep and a healthy breakfast. Sometimes being nervous means we stop taking care of ourselves.

Half an hour to go...
It's time to get into the right frame of mind. Get rid of distractions and find some time to focus. Take some deep breaths and picture yourself performing brilliantly. If you can see in your mind what success looks like, you're one step closer to getting there!

The curtain rises!
Once you're out there, believe in yourself. If you're prepared, you've done everything you need to do, and you can make it work. Good luck!

What are the heading and sub-headings in the text on the previous page?

Main heading: _____

Sub-heading 1: _____

Sub-heading 2: _____

Sub-heading 3: _____

Sub-heading 4: _____

Activity 2

1 | What do the sub-headings tell you?

- Where you should follow the advice ☐
- When you should follow the advice ☐
- Why you should follow the advice ☐

2 | How might these sub-headings help a reader? Explain your ideas.

_____

_____

_____

Activity 3

How helpful do you find the sub-headings? Explain your ideas.

_____

_____

_____

2: Adding headings

Activity 1

- Headings are words that appear as titles above pieces of writing.
- A heading tells the reader straight away what a piece of writing will be about.
- Some pieces of writing also have sub-headings.
- Sub-headings can help guide a reader through a piece of writing.

There are four short paragraphs in the piece of writing below. Look at each paragraph in turn, and think about what topic all the sentences are about. Add a sub-heading to each paragraph.

All about Elephants

_____

Elephants are the world's largest land animal. Male African elephants are the largest: they can reach three metres tall and weigh between 4,000 and 7,500 kilograms.

_____

In the wild, elephants live in in very hot areas of Africa and Asia. They live mainly in grass-lands and forests, but they are sometimes found in deserts or swamps, or on hilly land.

_____

Elephants eat **a lot**! An adult elephant eats up to 140 kilograms of food in a day. Elephants eat leaves, grass, roots, fruit and tree bark. They have to travel long distances to continue finding enough food.

_____

Elephants can get pretty old. Asian elephants can live up to 50 years. African elephants can live for almost as long as people: up to about 70 years!

Activity 2

The box below contains a short summary of the start of a story.

1 Add a title for the story as a whole.

2 Add a chapter heading for each chapter.

Title: _____

Chapter 1 heading: _____

The main character wakes up in a jungle. They have no idea where they are or how they got there. They start to explore their surroundings and find an ancient statue covered in jungle creepers. It looks like a giant woman with the head of a tiger.

Chapter 2 heading: _____

The main character sees something written on the base of the statue in a strange ancient language. They also see two carved images: one of a person with a treasure chest and one of a person running from tigers.

Chapter 3 heading: _____

The main character tries to search the area more, hoping there will be a clue to finding the treasure chest. They hear a distant rumbling coming nearer, but they keep searching. They find a stone covered in the same kind of writing as is on the statue, but with English underneath.

Chapter 4 heading: _____

The main character starts translating the writing on the statue using the writing on the stone. Leaves rustle nearby and the character realises the rumbling is actually a growl. They freeze: should they solve the puzzle or run?

Activity 3

Plan a piece of writing about different sports people enjoy.
Think about what topics you want to include. To make your plan,
write only the title and five sub-headings.

Title: _____

Sub-heading 1: _____

Sub-heading 2: _____

Sub-heading 3: _____

Sub-heading 4: _____

Sub-heading 5: _____

What do I Know?

1. I understand what headings and sub-headings are.

2. I understand how headings and sub-heading can be helpful.

3. I can add sub-headings and titles to different kinds of writing.

4. I can use headings and sub-headings to help me plan my own writing.

1: What is direct speech?

Activity 1

Punctuation guide

Dani said, "This is fun."

- Some sentences tell us what someone is saying. This is called speech.
- Speech goes inside **speech marks**. These are also called **inverted commas** because they look like upside-down commas.

Underline the speech in these sentences.

1. Fran says, "It is almost time for lunch."
2. Our teacher asked, "Does anyone have the answer?"
3. Mum shouted, "Come home!"
4. We called, "Hurry up!"
5. Enzo said, "It's getting dark already."

Activity 2

Punctuation guide

Dani said, "This is fun."

- The words next to speech can identify the **speaker** and should include a verb like 'to say'.
- When they come before the speech, these identifier words have a comma after them.
- Speech should start with a capital letter.
- The punctuation after speech should be inside the **speech marks**.

Tick the sentences that contain the correct punctuation and capital letters for speech.

1. Gran said, "Tidy your room!" ✓
2. My friend asked. Are you free this weekend? ☐
3. Moira calls, "Where is my book?" ☐
4. The headteacher says, "welcome to the school." ☐
5. Zoë and Jose say, "We will be at the park". ☐

Activity 3

Look again at the sentences you did not tick in Activity 2. Rewrite them, correcting the mistakes.

My friend asked, "Are you free this weekend?"

2: Starting to write speech

Activity 1

Punctuation guide

> Andrei asked, "Where is my jumper?"

- Some sentences include speech. The speech goes inside speech marks.
- The punctuation after speech should be inside the speech marks, too.

> Add speech marks to these sentences.

1. Xander says, "You can share my snack .

2. Rian calls, Wait for me and Tina !

Activity 2

Punctuation guide

- The words next to speech can identify the speaker and should include a verb like 'to say'.
- When they come before the speech, these identifier words have a comma after them.

1 Complete the sentences that describe this conversation.

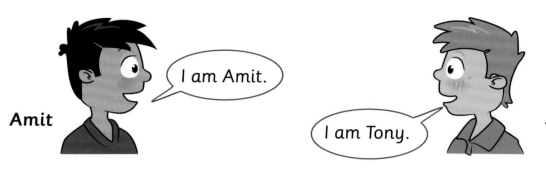

Amit says, "I am _____."

Tony says, "_____."

2 Write two sentences that describe this conversation.

_____

_____

Activity 3

Write one speech sentence of your own. You should add a name at the beginning.

_____ says _____

_____

_____

3: More ways to write speech

Activity 1

> Philipé said, "My tea is cold."

- Some sentences tell us someone's <u>speech</u>. The speech goes inside **speech marks**. These are also called **inverted commas**.
- **Words that identify the speaker** have a **comma** after them.
- Speech should start with a new **capital letter**.
- The **punctuation after speech** should be inside the **speech marks**.

> Complete this sentence using correctly punctuated speech.

Sarthak says __Today, I_____

Activity 2

> "My tea is cold," Philipé said. "Is your tea cold?" he asked. "It's freezing!" answered Amoli.

- Some punctuation changes when the **identifier words** come after the speech.
- The speech still starts with a **capital letter** but the **identifier** does not, unless it starts with a name or 'I'.
- In a **statement**, the speech has a **comma** after it, instead of a full stop. This goes inside the **speech marks**.
- In an **exclamation** or a **question**, the question mark or exclamation mark stays inside the **speech marks**.
- There is always a full stop at the end of the sentence, after the **identifier**.

Tick the sentences that contain the correct punctuation for speech.

- "Can we meet up tomorrow?" Dana asked. ☑
- "What do you think the weather will be like? Asked Tipi. ☐
- "The queue is so long." I sighed. ☐
- "Mine is the last house on the left," Sylvie said. ☐
- "Give back my doll!" cried Joey's little sister. ☐
- "Come here immediately" called Mum! ☐

Activity 3

Look again at the sentences you did not tick in Activity 2. Rewrite them, correcting the mistakes.

"What do think the weather will be like?" asked Tipi.

_____

_____

_____

4: Writing more speech

Activity 1

Punctuation guide

> "My tea is cold," Philipé said.
> "Is your tea cold?" asked Philipé.
> "It's freezing!" answered Amoli.

- Some sentences tell us someone's speech. The speech goes inside **speech marks**. New speech always starts with a capital letter.
- When the **identifier** comes after speech that is a **statement**, the speech has a comma after it. This goes inside the speech marks.
- When the **identifier** comes after speech that is an **exclamation** or a **question**, the question mark or exclamation mark stays inside the speech marks.
- There is always a full stop at the end of the sentence, after the **identifier**.

Add the correct punctuation to these sentences.

1. "Would you like to share these sandwiches Tom asked?

2. There is more paper in the cupboard Mr Tracey said.

Activity 2

Put each of these sentences into a longer speech sentence, with the identifier at the end.

1. I am tired. "I am tired," she said. _____

2. It is too hot. _____

   _____

3. I'm so thirsty! _____

   _____

4. What time is it? _____

   _____

Activity 3

Write a speech sentence of your own. Include an identifier that comes after the speech.

_____

_____

_____

What do I know?

1 I understand what direct speech is.

2 I know what punctuation to use when speech comes after identifier words.

3 I can punctuate and write speech sentences when speech comes after identifier words.

4 I know what punctuation to use when speech comes before identifier words.

5 I can punctuate and write speech sentences when speech comes before identifier words.

Here are some useful meanings. Key terms to understand are in orange.

Term	Meaning
Adjective	Adds information to a noun. It describes what the thing named is like. For example: 'the <u>red</u> dress'.
Adverbial	A word (an adverb) or phrase that adds information to an adjective, verb or other adverb. Many adverbs end '–ly', but not all of them. For example: 'I ran <u>quickly</u>. I was tired <u>almost as soon as I started</u>.'
Agreement	In a sentence, this means that all of the verb forms, nouns and other parts match together in the right ways, such as in their tenses.
Alphabet	All the letters in order from A to Z. A list of words in alphabetical order starts with letters that come first in the alphabet. For example: 'apple, ball, cat …'.
Apostrophe (')	A punctuation mark that can be used to show that letters have been missed out in a contraction or to show possession. For example: 'can't'; 'the horse's ears'.
Article	The words 'a', 'an', 'the' and 'some'. They are a type of determiner.
Auxiliary verb	Used to help create different forms of verbs. • Forms of 'to be' are used in progressive tenses. • Forms of 'to have' are used in perfect tenses. • For these verb forms the auxiliary verb changes to show tense and person.
Capital letter	Large versions of letters. They may also be formed differently. A capital letter is used at the start of a sentence or a name. For example: A, B, C.
Clause	A group of words, including a subject and a verb, that means one thing but is not a full sentence.

Term	Meaning
Comma (,)	A punctuation mark that can be used to separate items in a list and parts of a sentence that are not two clauses. It is often read as a short pause.
Command	A sentence that gives an instruction. Commands can be statements or exclamations, but they are never questions.
Compound	When two shorter words are joined together they make a compound word. For example: super + man = <u>superman</u>; play + ground = <u>playground</u>.
Conjunction	A word that links sentences together to form one longer sentence. In the new sentence, the original sentences become known as clauses.
Consonant	Any letter that is not a vowel.
Contraction	Words that have been shortened. Apostrophes in contractions show where letters have been missed out.
Coordinating conjunction	Links two main clauses in a sentence.
Definite determiner	A determiner that indicates something known and specific.
Demonstrative	There are four demonstratives: 'this', 'that', 'these' and 'those'. They can give basic information about whether something is singular ('this' and 'that') or plural ('these' and 'those'), and also about whether nearby ('this' and 'these') or far away ('that' and 'those'). They can be used as determiners or as pronouns.
Determiner	Positioned before nouns. They can give basic information about whether something is singular or plural and definite or indefinite. For example: '<u>two</u> boxes'; '<u>all of the</u> things'.
Direct speech	In writing, reports exactly what someone says. A sentence that includes direct speech will include the precise spoken words in speech marks (or 'inverted commas') and often an identifier.
Exclamation	A sudden cry that shows surprise, excitement or shock.
Exclamation mark (!)	A punctuation mark used at the end of a sentence to show that the sentence is an exclamation.

Term	Meaning
Expanded noun phrase	A noun phrase that includes extra information about the thing named by the noun, for example using an adjective.
Full stop (.)	A punctuation mark used at the end of a sentence, to show that the sentence is a statement.
Heading	Words that appear as titles above pieces of writing. A heading tells the reader straight away what a piece of writing is about.
Identifier	Used to name the speaker of direct speech and includes a verb such as 'to say'. For example: "Hello," said Gunther.
Indefinite determiner	A determiner that indicates something general and non-specific.
Infinitive verb	The most basic form of a verb is the infinitive. It is preceded by 'to' and expresses no tense and no person. For example: 'to walk'; 'to be'.
Inverted commas (" ") (' ')	Punctuation marks that show speech is being reported exactly. They are also known as speech marks. They can be double (" ") or single (' ').
Irregular	Words that do not follow rules when they change. Verbs can have irregular tenses. Nouns can have irregular plurals.
Letter	A symbol used for writing. A group of letters can make up a word.
List	A series of connected things. For example: 'In the pond, there are fish, frogs, toads and newts'.
Main clause	Gives the main point in a sentence. There can be more than one main clause in a sentence if they are equally important. If there are two main clauses joined by a conjunction in a sentence, swapping the order of two main clauses does not affect the meaning of the sentence.
Meaning	The thing or idea that a word, expression or sign represents.
Noun	A word that names a person, thing, event or idea.
Noun phrase	A group of words that all link to the thing named by the noun. A noun phrase can be as short as two words: a determiner and the noun.

Term	Meaning
Object	Something or someone that is involved in the action, but not doing the action. For example: 'Shanice plays the game.'
Paragraph	A clear section of a piece of writing, usually on the same topic. A new paragraph starts on a new line.
Past participle	A verb form used to form perfect tenses. A verb's past participle is usually the same as its past tense.
Past tense	A way of writing a verb to show that events or actions happened in the past.
Perfect tenses	Ways of writing a verb to show that an action is perfectly complete. They are formed with the auxiliary verb 'to have', which is the verb that changes to show tense and person, and a past participle.
Person	How a verb changes to show who or what does the action. Each person can be singular or plural. • The first person relates to oneself (for example, 'I', 'me'). • The second person relates to the direct recipient of a sentence (for example, 'you'). • The third person relates to another person or thing named in the sentence (for example, 'she', 'the cats').
Phrase	A group of words that means one thing but is not a full sentence. It could be as short as two words.
Plural	• For a noun it shows that there is more than one of a thing or person. • For a verb it shows that more than one person or thing is doing the action.
Possession	Means that something belongs to someone or something. This can mean it is owned by them or is related to them in a different way.
Possessive noun	A word that shows possession. The noun for the owner takes the possessive form. For singular nouns and plurals that do not end '–s', this is made up of the noun, an apostrophe and 's'. For plural nouns that end '–s', it is made up of the noun and an apostrophe.

Term	Meaning
Possessive pronoun	A word that stands in for a possessive noun. Possessive pronouns can be determiners (for example, 'my', 'your'). They can also be used independently to mean the possessive noun and the thing that is owned (for example, 'mine', 'yours').
Prefix	A group of letters added at the start of a word to change its meaning. For example: unhappy; replay.
Preposition	A word that makes links between parts of a sentence. It usually comes at the beginning of a prepositional phrase (for example, 'up the street', 'around the bend', 'with a big smile', 'after lunch'). A prepositional phrase can be parts of a noun phrase (for example, 'I live in the house up the street') or can be used as an adverbial (for example, 'I live up the street').
Present participle	A verb form ending '–ing'. Present participles are used to form progressive tenses.
Present tense	Ways of writing a verb to show that events or actions happen now or happen regularly.
Progressive tenses	Progressive tenses are ways of writing a verb to show that an action continues over a period of time. They are formed with the auxiliary verb 'is' (which changes to show tense and person), and a present participle.
Pronoun	A word that stands in for a noun or noun phrase. The words 'I', 'you' singular, 'he', 'she', 'it', 'we', 'you' plural and 'they' are all pronouns.
Punctuation	The marks made in writing that are not letters. Punctuation makes writing easier to understand.
Question	A sentence that is used to ask something. It ends with a question mark.
Question mark (?)	A punctuation mark used at the end of a sentence, in place of a full stop, to show that a sentence is a question.
Sentence	A group of words that means one whole thing. It gives a whole idea.
Singular	• For a noun it shows that there is only one thing or person. • For a verb it shows that only one person or thing is doing the action.

Term	Meaning
Speech marks (" ") (' ')	Punctuation marks that show speech is being reported exactly. They are also known as inverted commas. They can be double (" ") or single (' ').
Standard English	Standard English is English that is grammatically correct.
Statement	A sentence that ends with a full stop rather than a question mark or an exclamation mark. A statement gives a piece of information.
Sub-heading	Titles that are less important than the main title for a piece of writing. They appear before shorter sections and guide a reader through the piece of writing.
Subject	The person or thing doing an action. The subject carries out the action named by the verb.
Subordinate clause	Gives extra information that is not the key point in a sentence. There cannot be a subordinate clause in a sentence without a main clause. If a main clause and a subordinate clause are joined by a conjunction in a sentence, swapping their positions affects the meaning or makes no sense.
Subordinating conjunction	Links a main clause to a subordinate clause in a sentence.
Suffix	A letter or group of letters added at the end of a word to change its meaning. For example: farm<u>ing</u>; farm<u>er</u>.
Tense	Shows when the action happens.
Verb	The name of an action. Every sentence must contain at least one verb.
Vowel	The letters 'a', 'e', 'i', 'o' and 'u'.
Word	A group of spoken sounds or written letters that make up one unit of meaning. In slow speech, a word has silence on each side of it. In writing, it has a space on each side of it.
Word family	A word family is a group of words with the same root word and related spellings. For example: 'farm', 'farmer', 'farming' and 'farmed'; 'please', 'displeasing', 'pleasant' and 'pleasantries'.

Adverbials

1: What are adverbials?

Activity 1

1. in the morning [underlined]
2. during lunch break [underlined]
3. with great excitement [underlined]

Activity 2

1. on Saturday [underlined]; time
2. To stay dry [underlined]; cause
3. every day [underlined]; time
4. at the weekend [underlined]; time
5. as a result of my good work [underlined]; cause

Activity 3

1. looked [circled]; with a frown [underlined]; adverbial phrase
2. cycled [circled]; in quite a rush [underlined]; adverbial phrase
3. bright [underlined]; pink [circled]; adverb
4. surprisingly [underlined]; busy [circled]; adverb

2: Adding adverbials

Activity 1

1a–b. [Children's answers will vary, but each must add an appropriate adverbial phrase to each sentence.]
2. for his birthday; to cheer him up

Activity 2

1–4. [Children's answers will vary, but each must add an appropriate adverb or adverbial phrase to each sentence. Between all questions, one adverbial of time and one adverbial of cause must be used.]

Activity 3

1. [Children's answers will vary, but each must include an adverb.]
2. [Children's answers will vary, but each must include an adverbial phrase.]

Demonstratives

1: What are demonstrative determiners?

Activity 1

- We are close to the station now. [ticked]
- All of the boxes were used. [ticked]
- I cycle but the other pupils walk. [ticked]

Activity 2

1. These [underlined]; plural [ticked]; near [ticked]
2. Those [underlined]; plural [ticked]; far [ticked]
3. that [underlined]; singular [ticked]; far [ticked]
4. This [underlined]; singular [ticked]; near [ticked]

Activity 3

this; These; That; those [each underlined]

2: Using demonstrative determiners

Activity 1

1. this; 2. that; 3. these; 4. those

Activity 2

1. These; 2. that; 3. this; 4. those

Activity 3

[Children's answers will vary, but each should include the demonstrative determiner shown below.]
1. 'this'; 2. 'that'; 3. 'these'; 4. 'those'

3: What are demonstrative pronouns?

Activity 1
1. paintings; these [each underlined]
2. Jared; he [each underlined]
3. This; book [each underlined]
4. Misaki and Miu; them [each underlined]
5. that; end [each underlined]
6. sweets; those [each underlined]

Activity 2
1. That idea was a good idea.
2. Most jumpers are too short for me, but this jumper fits okay.
3. Fran made many of the models, but Jake made those models.
4. These biscuits are the biscuits we made in class today.

Activity 3
1. (The) stew; some [each underlined]
2. (his) tasks; any [each underlined]
3. soup; (or) pasta; neither [each underlined]

4: Using demonstrative pronouns

Activity 1
1. this; 2. that; 3. those; 4. these

Activity 2
1. If I carry these dishes, can you carry those?
2. I know you wanted Aimee's book, but read this instead.
3. Everyone needs a paint brush. Can you hand out these?
4. John had a great idea – I wish I had thought of that.

Activity 3
1. one / some
2. most / none / plenty / one / some
3. much

Possession

1: Exploring more possessive nouns

Activity 1
1. Marc's kitten
2. my brother's clothes
3. the mountain's highest peak

Activity 2
1a. Owners: children; parents
   Things belonging to them: laughter; attention
1b. Owners: jugglers; men
   Things belonging to them: balls; feet
2a. The doctors' skill saved those men's lives.
2b. The children's workbooks were in the teachers' cupboards.

Activity 3
Grass's ability to get nutrients is improved by earthworms' tunnels.

2: Spotting possessive pronouns

Activity 1
- I; We; them; They; she; him [each underlined]

Activity 2
- Object pronouns:
  me; you; him; her; it; us; you; them
- Possessive determiners:
  my; your; his; her; its; our; your; their
- Independent possessive pronouns:
  mine; yours; his; hers; its; ours; yours; theirs

Activity 3
our; her; Ours; my; yours; your; mine; his; their; theirs [each underlined]

3: What are possessive determiners?

Activity 1
all of the; some; two; a; my; a few
[each underlined]

Activity 2
1. Our; my; your; his; their; its; her
   [each underlined]
2. our   – Nadia and Pietr's
   my   – Nadia's
   your – Nadia's
   his   – Pietr's
   their – Tammie and Jack's
   its   – the bus's
   her   – the driver's

Activity 3
1. my; your; His; its; her
   [each underlined twice in the
   Activity 2 story]
2. Our; their [each circled in the
   Activity 2 story]

4: Using possessive determiners

Activity 1
1. her shoes
2. his lesson plan
3. its steering wheel

Activity 2
1. his; her
2. their
3. its
4. our
5. your; my

Activity 3
1. Get out your crayons.
2. The judges announced their
   decision.
3. This is our house.

5: What are independent possessive pronouns?

Activity 1
loads; none; these; any
[each underlined]

Activity 2
1. Ours; mine; theirs; His; hers; Yours
2. mine   –   Ginny's book
   yours –   Ginny's book
   his   –   Tim's book
   hers   –   Sun-Yin's book
   ours   –   Sheila's and Dom's books
   theirs –   Tim's and Sun-Yin's books

Activity 3
1. mine; yours; His; hers
   [each underlined twice in the
   Activity 2 story]
2. Ours; theirs
   [each circled in the Activity 2 story]

6: Using independent possessive pronouns

Activity 1
our project – ours
your idea – yours
their display – theirs
my work – mine
his plan – his
its facts – its
her speech – hers

Activity 2
1. yours; mine
2. hers
3. his
4. its
5. ours; theirs

Activity 3
1. The pictures are on display. Mine is in
   the middle.

2. Can I get my hair cut? I want it to look like hers.

3. Our house is opposite theirs.

7: Choosing possessive pronouns

Activity 1
- Object pronouns:
  me; you; him; her; it; us; you; them
- Possessive determiners:
  my; your; his; her; its; our; your; their
- Independent possessive pronouns:
  mine; yours; his; hers; its; ours; yours; theirs

Activity 2
1. her; yours [underlined]
2. My; their [underlined]
3. mine; hers [underlined]
4. your; ours [underlined]
5. our; theirs [underlined]

Activity 3
[Children's answers will vary but each should include the following.]
1. 'its' used as a possessive determiner
2. 'his' used as an independent possessive pronoun

Prepositions

1: What are prepositions?

Activity 1
- a very young child [underlined]
- my grandfather [underlined and circled]
- an enormous sweet jar [underlined]
- his kitchen [underlined and circled]
- some toffees [underlined and circled]
- chewy mints [underlined]
- bright red lollipops [underlined]

Activity 2
1. at [circled, underlined]; the lesson at 9 o'clock [underlined]
2. with [circled]; the man with the long white beard [underlined]
3. at [circled]; the food at her local restaurant [underlined]
4. due to [circled]; our day off due to snow [underlined]
5. up to [circled]; Her time up to noon [underlined]

Activity 3
1. The film about sea monsters was my favourite. [ticked]
2. The fish in the tank swam up to the surface. [ticked]
3. Mr Jones was accepting donations for the school trip. [ticked]

2: What are prepositional phrases?

Activity 1
1. by my favourite author [underlined]
2. in tennis [underlined]
3. on Sundays [underlined]
4. of the audience [underlined]

Activity 2
1. the day before yesterday [underlined]
2. the bared teeth of the snarling tiger [underlined]
3. the bright, flashing reflection in the window of the house [underlined]
4. a new school far from her friends [underlined]
5. Your whispers during the film [underlined]

Activity 3
1. the day; 2. the teeth; 3. the reflection; 4. a school; 5. your whispers

3: Using prepositional phrases

Activity 1
through; of; in; on; for; at

Activity 2
[Children's answers will vary, but each must add adjectives and prepositional phrases to each of the six noun phrases.]

Activity 3
[Children's answers will vary.]

More conjunctions

1: Revising clauses and conjunctions

Activity 1
1. 9 / Nine / nine
2. and; so; but; because; or

Activity 2
1. I wanted to stay up but I'm too tired.
2–5. [Children's answers will vary, but each must be a sentence that includes one of the given conjunctions not used elsewhere in the activity.]

Activity 3
[Children's answers will vary, but their responses to Activity 2 should be annotated with underlining beneath each clause.]

2: More subordinating conjunctions

Activity 1
- I'd left my bag at home so I had to return for it. [ticked]
- Dina was keen to finish the game because she'd almost won. [ticked]

Activity 2
1. although; 2. if; 3. so;
4. when; 5. after

Activity 3
1. I had studied before I took part. [underlined]
2. I have work to do after I get home, though. [underlined]

3: Writing subordinate clauses

Activity 1
1. she had to give a speech.
2–3. [Children's answers will vary, but each must add an appropriate subordinate clause.]

Activity 2
1–3. [Children's answers will vary, but each must be a sentence that includes a conjunction not used elsewhere in the activity.]

Activity 3
[Children's answers will vary, but each must rewrite one sentence from Activity 2 with a different conjunction and subordinate clause.]

Verb forms

1: Exploring simple tenses

Activity 1
1. made; 2. cooked; 3. hurried;
4. traced; 5. travelled; 6. were

Activity 2
1. to be; 2. to have; 3. to go;
4. to come; 5. to find; 6. to fly;
7. to sleep; 8. to speak

Activity 3

[Each answer should be written as a label on Activity 2.]
1. third person singular
2. third person plural
3. third person singular
4. second person plural
5. first person singular
6. second person singular
7. first person plural
8. third person singular

2: Practising verb agreement

Activity 1

begin; saw; talks; leave; was
[each underlined]

Activity 2

1. I knew it was your birthday, so I planned ahead and went to your party. You had such a surprise, which made me smile.
2. Her dream is this: she meets her grandfather, and he says he has an adventure ahead of him. Then he rises into the air and flies.

Activity 3

forgot; skipped; is; am; made; says; does

3: What are perfect tenses?

Activity 1

1. have [circled]; talked [underlined]
2. had [circled]; recovered [underlined]
3. has [circled]; been [underlined]
4. had [circled]; arrived [underlined]
5. has [circled]; left [underlined]

Activity 2

1. has caught [underlined]; present perfect

2. had finished [underlined]; past perfect
3. had frozen [underlined]; past perfect
4. has known [underlined]; present perfect
5. has worn [underlined]; present perfect

Activity 3

- I have heard his new song. [ticked]
- are [underlined]
- I had forgotten about the test. [ticked]
- We have run all the way here. [ticked]
- had [underlined]
- Lida had hoped for a new bike. [ticked]

[NB: 'had' is a correctly formed verb, but not a correctly formed perfect verb.]

4: Forming perfect verbs

Activity 1

1. finished
2–4. [Children's answers will vary, but each must make sense in context.]

Activity 2

1a. Basia has arrived. She has waved to us.
1b. I have been waiting for a train. It has rained all night.
2a. Basia had arrived. She had waved to us.
2b. I had been waiting for a train. It had rained all night.

Activity 3

1. [Children's answers will vary, but each must be a sentence containing the past-perfect verb form 'had been'.]
2. [Children's answers will vary, but each must be a sentence containing the past-perfect verb form 'has said' or 'have said'.]

Headings for paragraphs

1: What are headings?

Activity 1
- Main heading:
  Preparing to Perform on Stage
- Sub-heading 1: Before the big day
- Sub-heading 2: The day itself!
- Sub-heading 3: Half an hour to go…
- Sub-heading 4: The curtain rises!

Activity 2
1. When you should follow the advice [ticked]
2. [Children's answers will vary, but they should acknowledge that the sub-headings help to sequence the paragraphs and/or allow a reader to see quickly which piece of the advice to follow at any one time.]

Activity 3
[Children's answers will vary, but should be explained and justified.]

2: Adding headings

Activity 1
[Children's answers will vary slightly but must suit the topic of each paragraph:
- how big elephants are
- where elephants live
- what elephants eat
- how old elephants can get]

Activity 2
[Children's answers will vary, but should make sense in relation to the chapters' content.]

Activity 3
[Children's answers will vary, but should include a title that's relevant to the subject of sports and five logical headings for topics within it.]

Direct speech

1: What is direct speech?

Activity 1
1. It is almost time for lunch. [underlined]
2. Does anyone have the answer? [underlined]
3. Come home! [underlined]
4. Hurry up! [underlined]
5. It's getting dark already. [underlined]

Activity 2
- Gran said, "Tidy your room!" [ticked]
- Moira calls, "Where is my book?" [ticked]

Activity 3
- My friend asked, "Are you free this weekend?"
- The headteacher says, "Welcome to the school."
- Zoë and Jose say, "We will be at the park."

2: Starting to write speech

Activity 1
1. Xander says, "You can share my snack."
2. Rian calls, "Wait for me and Tina!"

Activity 2
1. Amit says, "I am Amit."
   Tony says, "I am Tony."
2. Kisha says, "Can I help you?"
   Pam says, "Yes! I am lost!"

[Children may use different identifier verbs if they are correctly formed.]

Activity 3
[Children's answers will vary, but each must be a correctly punctuated speech sentence.]

3: More ways to write speech
Activity 1 [Children's answers will vary, but each must be a correctly punctuated speech sentence.]
Activity 2 • "Can we meet up tomorrow?" Dana asked. [ticked] • "Mine is the last house on the left," Sylvie said. [ticked] • "Give back my doll!" cried Joey's little sister. [ticked]
Activity 3 • "What do you think the weather will be like?" asked Tipi. • "The queue is so long," I sighed. • "Come here immediately!" called Mum.

4: Writing more speech
Activity 1 1. "Would you like to share these sandwiches?" Tom asked. 2. "There is more paper in the cupboard," Mr Tracey said.
Activity 2 [Children's choices of identifiers will vary, but the identifiers' position and each sentence's punctuation must be as in the answers below.] 1. "I am tired," she said. 2. "It is too hot," she said. 3. "I'm so thirsty!" she cried. 4. "What time is it?" she asked.
Activity 3 [Children's answers will vary, but must be correctly punctuated speech sentences with the identifier after the speech.]